Volume 114 of the Yale Series of Younger Poets

The Solace Is Not the Lullaby

JILL OSIER

Foreword by Carl Phillips

Yale UNIVERSITY PRESS

New Haven and London

Published with assistance from a grant to honor James Merrill.

Yale University Press books may be purchased in quantity for educational, business, or promotional use. For information, please e-mail sales.press@yale.edu (U.S. office) or sales@yaleup.co.uk (U.K. office).

Set in Fournier type by Integrated Publishing Solutions.
Printed in the United States of America.

Library of Congress Control Number: 2019947998
ISBN 978-0-300-25035-0 (hardcover : alk. paper)
ISBN 978-0-300-25034-3 (paperback : alk. paper)

A catalogue record for this book is available from the British Library.

This paper meets the requirements of ANSI/NISO Z39.48-1992 (Permanence of Paper).

10 9 8 7 6 5 4 3 2 1

for my mother and father

Contents

Foreword

Late in Jill Osier's *The Solace Is Not the Lullaby*—a model of clarity and of the powers of brevity, as well as, more subtly, a quiet but no less persuasive interrogation of what we mean anymore by words like "knowing," "confession," "story," maybe even "poetry" itself—we encounter the following:

> Something else beautiful:
> I remembered, the town I'm from,
> people there went about their day
> and work as if they thought
> no one was watching.
>
> ("Storm of the Century")

It's a reminder that the book began with trespass, and that someone has indeed been watching, all along. Here's that opening poem, "Small Town," in its entirety:

> Listen. The rug is wet because
> I stood here. Because
> it started pouring. Because
> your door was open and I was
> under a tree. Because
> it was raining. Because the rain
> and tree both
> were in your backyard. Because
> so was I. Because you
> weren't home. Because I knew
> you were bowling. Because
> I walk your road. Because your road
> goes by your house. Because
> I felt like a walk. Because

it was going to rain. Because your door
is never locked.

There's a slightly sinister, stalkerlike quality to the sensibility here, but that turns out to be not at all where Osier is headed with these poems. Yes, the speaker in this particular poem has indeed entered someone's house while the owner was away, and has clearly spent a lot of time observing that person's habits of coming and going. But Osier's larger concern is with the half-involuntary trespass which is just each of us encroaching on one another's lives, which is to say coexisting and therefore necessarily intersecting with the lives of others, sometimes deliberately, sometimes by the accident of happening to live in the same town. For the most part, the town in these poems is a small, unnamed one in the Midwest, in which the usual things occur: death, sex, an auction, children at play, adults longing for love, adults trying to remember the past and characteristically finding only pieces of it "almost there, almost / gone" ("Kansas"). Osier's task—as is always the task of poetry—is to look past that quotidian surface that most of us hold tightly to, lest we have to see more than we can bear.

Osier's mind works like the light she describes in "Homage," like "a broom of thought / pushing up into an attic for the secret and abandoned." I'd have expected the poems, accordingly, to lay secrets bare, and to give something like home again to the abandoned. Instead, Osier tends to be more interested in the abandonment itself, and to give us just a piece of what, in the end, remains as secret as ever. The point seems to be neither rescue nor mere revelation—both, in their ways, forms of certainty—but to reinforce what can be a difficult truth for our empirically minded human selves: that, despite our longing for proof and stability, for the form that gives shape (and therefore meaning) to shapelessness, "the hollow more than shape is certain" ["Some Roads in Iowa (II)"]. Here's a brief example of Osier's method:

Story

It might have happened
at the river, petting the wild swan,

the pure-breasted, black-eyed silent one
drawing us down in our dresses and suits
through branches and mud to banks
wet and hidden.

Because of all the lovely details of the swan, the seductive movement of the
poem as it tracks the swan's ability to seduce the speaker and company
farther into a natural interior, not worrying about their clothing despite the
mud and wet, it takes a moment for me to realize that the initial "It" never
gets identified. One possibility is that the "It" is some event that itself
never gets disclosed but instead discloses—via displacement—a detail of
the event's *context*: X is whatever *might* have happened while the following
things *definitely* happened.

The "It" could, alternatively, refer to the title. The *story* is what might
have happened. But that leaves us no less in the dark, since we're never
told the story. My hunch is that Osier at some level wants us to rethink our
ideas about story itself. We're used to a tradition of story as beginning,
middle, and end (resolution); and even in our post-postmodern age (if that's
the name for it), in which fragment is hardly a surprise, the impulse more
often than not is to navigate backward from fragment to an at least imag-
ined, possible story of which the fragment is clear evidence. But what if,
Osier suggests, the fragment *is* the story—or more sobering, will have to
be, because it's all we've got?

On one hand this question concerns epistemology. It suggests that
knowing is not so much about the possession of facts that might establish a
truth, something certain, but more about accepting that knowing is itself,
inherently, to do with what can never be known. To put it more exactly,
knowing may well be mostly mystery, not the clearing up of mystery. Or
as Osier puts it, "Certainty always stands closest / to no thing we have"
("Lake Saganaga"). "Ice Boat Notes" opens with authoritative declaration,
and goes on to suggest that the speaker knows whereof she speaks, because
of the supposed evidence she next presents. Here's the poem:

The seasons are always beating us
to the best ideas. This one's spectrum

siphons to bare, to a naked release
of birds. I know. I followed them
like clues, all the way to where the ground
gets shy, dipping down to little creeks, and a huge gray
tank was already there, rusting in the forest like a submarine.

But notice how, immediately after the confidence of "I know," the speaker
follows the birds, which are "like clues," which is to say they're *not* clues,
they only resemble them. Be that as it may, where these cluelike birds lead
to is a space that contains a rusting tank—maybe a water tank of some sort,
maybe (given the connotations of "submarine") a military tank. It's not
clear. But alongside the mysteries of what kind of a tank this is, what it's
doing in the landscape, who it once belonged to, and how any of this proves
anything of the poem's earlier statements—alongside all this, Osier offers
at least a couple of fragments of fact: the ground dips, which is understood
in terms of human personality, as "the ground / gets shy"; and there's a
tank, made by humans but devoid of personality. Something, then, is being
suggested about humankind and the natural world—the ways in which they
overlap, how each can differently contain the other, but also how each can
become the other or take on traces of it, until knowing itself can get con-
founded: as Randall Jarrell now almost long ago put it, "Which one's the
mockingbird? which one's the world?" Certain mysteries—most of them—
remain mysteries in an Osier poem; but, as here, we more often than not
end up with an invitation to live *inside* a particular mystery, to meditate
on it. It feels oddly, incongruously (dare I say magically?) like closure, a
steady place to land.

But if epistemology is part of Osier's concerns in these poems, another
concern is where to situate oneself as a poet, when it comes to narrative
and confession and to the relationship between the two. Osier tends to
begin with an apparent subject—often in medias res—only to leave it be-
hind for another, concluding subject or image that raises any number of
new subjects, none of which gets resolved. The risk, of course, is frustra-
tion, on the reader's part—but if frustration, I'd call it a meaningful, delib-
erate one, insofar as the poems enact how the mind and, more largely, life
itself work. Meaningful, too, in that it forces us to engage with the poem

differently than we'd expected: as we saw with "Ice Boat Notes," what might seem either a didactic or narrative poem turns out to be more of an open meditation, or an invitation to one. At other times Osier's poems use this strategy in order to make us question assumed hierarchies of importance, and/or to show us how the mind attempts to defer what's more difficult by focusing on what is less so. Here's "The Horses Are Fighting":

> They stand scattered and not
> facing each other. Like black-eyed
> susans lining the highway, or sisters
> angry in some small kitchen.
>
> The goats, they traipse a diagonal
> through knee-high meadow,
> following head to tail. Then
> one decides to feed. Suddenly
> they are strangers.
>
> But how elegant animals seem
> these weeks after your funeral, each
> quiet despite a whole field, content
> with any fresh mouthful.

I can easily imagine a workshop in which the poet is advised to cut the first two stanzas, to begin with the funeral reference, and to tell us more about the you of the poem and the speaker's relationship to said you. But so many useful points are getting made in this poem. Questions like what's more important: what's happening right now, or a death that occurred weeks ago? Also, we're reminded here how in the wake of loss we often have an impulse to speak *around* that loss rather than toward it. Meanwhile the poem shows how casually death enters any given picture, and how unexpectedly. Another point: that the natural world has its own, often unparsable geometry—the goats as they "traipse a diagonal," death as it simultaneously runs parallel to and will eventually encircle all of the above (our speaker included), and who's to say the scatteredness of those horses is not its own resistance to our human assumptions when it comes to pattern?

But there's also this business of confession and narrative to which I alluded earlier, and which is really at the heart of workshop suggestions like the one I imagined. After all our sophistication, we humans still love a story, often one that unfolds in ways that are counter to how life actually unfolds. Story as escape sometimes; other times as a road to clarity at least, even if what's clear turns out to be difficult to look too long upon. Consistent, I hope, with what I said earlier about fragment as story in Osier's work, I wonder too whether Osier is suggesting that we often ask the wrong questions. Instead of What is the story, Osier asks What is tellable, how much is tellable? This is especially worth thinking about if we agree with Osier that knowledge itself never lies far from mystery. How to speak, for example, about love, if "we are never loving what we think we are," which implies that our thinking is itself untrustworthy—how then to understand the object of our thinking, let alone of our love ("Some Roads in Iowa")? As for confession, that more personal version of story—at least traditionally—in which we reveal what's hidden within ourselves, it's interesting to me that Osier's speaker tends to observe what's around her, rather than to divulge what's inside. If there are confessions, they tend to get made in a slant fashion, as in this stanza from "Mars":

> Something happened today,
> an honesty I may have missed
> except I was swimming
> in a small-town river. This river,
> like any other, has had its chances,
> has taken all of them. Today
> I thought I saw it reconsider.

Clearly, rivers can't reconsider anything, or consider, for that matter. What this feels more persuasively like is that the *speaker* has come to have regrets about *her own* chances that she had, once, and took, or possibly didn't. The implication is that there's something like regret, or at least a taking stock of one's choices, and not being altogether certain how to feel about how they've ended. This stanza occurs in one of the book's longer poems (at six stanzas), and seems to have been dropped into the poem by chance, incidentally, surrounded by other stanzas that discuss family and some isolated incidents in the family history. To what effect?

I think Osier is trying to say something here about modesty as one way, perhaps the most honest one, to conduct a human life. It's not that there aren't things to confess; rather, our human travails are finally facts, inescapable, and they finally mean very little, despite how powerfully they resonate within each of us. What is a death in the family—doesn't the world continue? So we regret some of our choices—but we made them, they're not erasable, and the stars appear at night anyway. It's not that we don't matter; and it is. Is this the knowledge—the certainty—we were so keen, all this time, to reach?

All the contemporary world's noise and possibilities—for better and worse—notwithstanding, most of us live quiet enough lives, or want to, quiet and modest, hoping to do as little harm as possible, hoping to *be* harmed as little as possible. Osier's poems don't shy from the inevitable losses and regrets—and other mysteries—that attend a life. But together the poems also argue, it seems to me, that to live modestly is not the worst way, is in fact a way of maintaining a useful perspective on such things as loss and regret—of seeing our lives as both resonant and limited, as fragments, rather like memory, which is to say, like knowing. Note that modesty doesn't have to mean powerless; Dickinson's poems, too, are modest. Nor does modesty here in any way compromise ambition. To the poems of Jill Osier's *The Solace Is Not the Lullaby*, there's a quiet, cumulative, inescapable power that gets deployed via restraint and precision. Osier knows full well that the risk of clarity is "mere" transparency, yet she trusts in clarity, even as she trusts, too, in what might be life's clearest truth: that it's all mostly mystery. Clear, yet rife with nuance, enigmatic, these poems announce what must suffice, and they do so beautifully: *"We have seen every edge,* they say, */ and you were right"* ("The Steps in the Snow Lead Around and Around a Place Called Want").

CARL PHILLIPS

THE SOLACE IS NOT THE LULLABY

Small Town

Listen. The rug is wet because
I stood here. Because
it started pouring. Because
your door was open and I was
under a tree. Because
it was raining. Because the rain
and tree both
were in your backyard. Because
so was I. Because you
weren't home. Because I knew
you were bowling. Because
I walk your road. Because your road
goes by your house. Because
I felt like a walk. Because
it was going to rain. Because your door
is never locked.

Some Roads in Iowa

He lived down the street, on a dead end
known as Boulevard. A quiet boy I grew up
drawn to, he grew lean, curving hard
and away like a good pitch
or trout.

We are never loving what we think we are. Never
simply. The first thing we loved
we don't even remember: a corner
of fabric, some handle. When we loved again,
perhaps a sound, we were actually trying to hear
fabric. We listened for corners.

This Field Wasn't Always a Field

The paint on the hood glistens.
If she looks deep, glints of light like fish
or stars start swimming. She thinks
she's seen this before in nail polish.
She smells her fingers, checks the middle one's
last knuckle. Swollen. A crescent purpled
one side this morning. Some grounder's
bad hop she doesn't remember. The boy's still
trying to say it, leaned back on the windshield, but all
the Irish blood in the ground can't help. Quiet, quiet,
all the way home. He corners carefully
like someone older. In two years she will learn
to drive. Her temple rests in one small circle
on the window, all the blood leaving there,
a cold coming in.

Fall

Before there was a pink sky
there was a jet-white horse
and lip-soiled stationery promising
rides. There were so many ways
to go up! And dresses waiting. Men
had beards, were judged by them. Where
was fear, where was it? *Check*
my purse. Check and see
if the neighbors have any. I heard *no,*
I must have, but I heard it
like thunder: not right away,
not until later.

Edge of the World

The summer my grandmother was dying my father walked me
to a carnival so my mother could sob into the living room carpet. It was
the last summer I wore red bib overalls and the red and white sailor shirt—
the summer I couldn't quite see past the logic of baseball, so after
the Babe Ruth boys took the championship, Toya Nelson and I
went looking for them. She invited herself places, which made
my mother kind of sad, but I just thought she wasn't afraid,
and what was sad about that? Her brothers had pounded this
into her, liked to string her up in a backyard tree by her feet. We
found the team at Jason Raisty's, jerseys damp, their bangs stuck
to dirty foreheads. We all sat with legs touching, watching movies
that made you squeeze your knees together, look at your hands. I
thought about hook slides. The air outside was big and quiet when we left.
I walked her home to her mother's trailer, to sleep curled next to her, her cowlick
and crooked jaw, her stubby fingers and coppery skin, her breasts always two
years behind mine.

Some Roads in Iowa (II)

What toy, looking back, taught me wrong? It said
to pull apart its hemispheres, let its insides
tumble out. It said to fill the hollowness again,
matching pieces to same-shaped holes. My
many-eyed pumpkin. My few-starred sky.

I was still a girl. I watched my left foot step
into what would be a shape, saw hips
then hands follow. I left sleep for concrete
outside his basement bedroom window
and sat at the screen for the sound of his breathing.

The hollow more than shape is certain,
unfinished as some roads in Iowa
—or childhood, where the sounds started,
where we listened hard.

II

Story

It might have happened
at the river, petting the wild swan,
the pure-breasted, black-eyed silent one
drawing us down in our dresses and suits
through branches and mud to banks
wet and hidden.

Grip

The children are defending a sandbar.
The rocks they hold above their heads are large
wishes hitting the water. They do not need
to be home until dark. The trailer sits back
from a bend in the river, its front yard a puzzle
like one they found at a rummage sale once,
free since pieces were missing. Only things
like ice and snow come back. Soon the sky
will leave the river alone, won't play with it.
They've watched this happen again and again.
They've told no one.

From

Sometimes the light,
as we all sat down to supper,
was, briefly, the very blue
of our collars.

We took this
in every weather
as warmth.

Later I felt us pulling
something up against the wind
of those who seemed to know
an easier way.

Lake Saganaga

And the whole time we fished, wishes
lined up the way shadows
refuse to. It ended up being the perfect time
for them to do this: we were all still
remembering ourselves as a family, and the light was
as it is when you trust it will hold, good enough
to know you may have had something
but lost it. Certainty always stands closest
to no thing we have.

Of Unsent Letters, One

The man who bought the field has horses,
and they're out there now, fenced wide and loosely.
And I've been upset over the whole thing,
losing the silo pit (why have I clung to a stone
ring all these years?), but now I admit
I love to see them. I've never owned a horse.
I don't remember, fully, the last time I was on one,
but they fill, nonetheless, an emptiness.
There are several places at the edge of town
where horses are kept:
two in the pasture by the river, two more
behind the barn on Stockyard Street,
a young mare who walks the fence with me
along the gravel road, a restless one
bucking in his own circles off the old highway,
two watching as I head out toward the cemetery,
and now these—there are three—behind my house.
I find I want to watch them all the time.
It seems more important than anything else
I could be doing right now. When the sun
comes up over the hill, they are there,
perfect and restful. When I come home,
they are grazing, still oblivious. I go out
while their backs have the moon on them,
the air thick, my feet wet with alfalfa. At night
they are the darkest shadows in the field.

Kansas

It's midnight in Kansas.
The mother goes to wake the daughter.
The ballplayer's bruises rise to the surface.
Heat has held the daughter, and trees
are bent over in the yard, not from snow.
The girl rises and bends,
tying her shoes in the kitchen's dark.
The grandmother has tied bricks to the ends
of the branches.
No one is on the road.
The fields sweat into the air, a mild stew.
The ballplayer rolls over. His sheets are wet.
Mother and daughter come from the garage
leading bony bikes.
The grandmother goes to the quilt.
The girl's arms reach for handlebars.
Pedaling hard, she can imagine wind.
There are stars. This is as dark
intended. This is as light
as she will be.
The ballplayer snores softly, one hand
badly scuffed.
The quilt, unfinished, is already
heavier than the air.
She pedals faster, and the trees look
like they never do drawn, wind
more and more like her mother's
voice, almost there, almost
gone. Hung on the wall, the quilt
would sag like a carcass being drained.
It could smother a body like a body.

Dirge

At the home today
Ardis wears a colorful dress,
and I fix her collar like a wife
before church.

Meanwhile, the town bakes
in its thick air and dust, its scent
of rotting grain.

My father comes home from work
a ghost. Pink flakes nest in his hair
and edge our linoleum. I pick
hot golden kernels from the dryer.

In gutters downtown,
young stalks wave green
almost knee-high in spare dirt,
trying to get away with it.
Corn is ambitious.

Without

Blue rose of a shirt crumpled,
the neck with two wrists
asleep in its scent. After rain,
I'd like no needs to wake.

But weeds in the dying man's garden
wait. The bee to be dethroned again.
Onions tangle like suspicion, slowly
with their rotting arms.

And the only fire is the sun
some nights. It goes dutiful
as a child might. *Now go,*
and leave the door closed this time.

The Horses Are Fighting

They stand scattered and not
facing each other. Like black-eyed
susans lining the highway, or sisters
angry in some small kitchen.

The goats, they traipse a diagonal
through knee-high meadow,
following head to tail. Then
one decides to feed. Suddenly
they are strangers.

But how elegant animals seem
these weeks after your funeral, each
quiet despite a whole field, content
with any fresh mouthful.

On Death

I might have guessed,
running the streets that night,

running each right
down the middle, not

meeting a car, rain soaking
and so soft, my arms

held out for the last
corner to the house,

that the dark figure
sitting on the porch swing

would be my mother,
the night and storm

and night's storm
like a sentence

she could no longer be
subject or object for.

III

Mars

It's as if I sit on my overturned bucket
in the middle of the grass and watch,
from a distance, a garden rot.

For years it did not haunt me like this,
the image of my siblings in the rows, my sister
all brown in a tube top, my little brother sometimes
just missing. It would get hotter, my mother
insisted, so, morning sun on us, we picked.

Something happened today,
an honesty I may have missed
except I was swimming
in a small-town river. This river,
like any other, has had its chances,
has taken all of them. Today
I thought I saw it reconsider.

A clear, sunlit day is hard
in the way it is full with itself,
not waiting for you.
The river, it turns out,
is not waiting.

It was sunny the day
my mother left, taking my brother
in the heavy black-and-white
checkered stroller. There was sun
at the curb where I finally stopped
and studied close the makeup
of concrete.

Tonight, bodies will shine
with old light. Some will never
be this close again.

Relume

It is not morning but the very other side of morning
when the birthday boy tries to rake from the river
balloons he'd thrown in brick-tied,
angry at his sister. Their color now at dusk,
as they float like a family of pink soup bowls upturned, blooms
hard in his chest.

There are maybe two ways
you could make this town smaller.
Cut off everyone's feet
or close one eye.

A woman mowed her lawn
for years—tube-topped
in terry cloth, hair in scarf—
atop a red Snapper.

She wore dangly earrings, punching
perfect rows of circles in kids'
school lunch tickets.

She married, adopted,
divorced, all the time mowing
her large lawn on the edge
of a little town.

She was slender and did sweatpants
a favor. Even her feet
were brown—red
Snapper goddess!

I am standing on her clean
sheared grass, bidding
to a jabbering cowboy
hat. There are tricks
to this: don't scratch

your head, hide your interest,
stay cool against dealers looming
coon-eyed and fat. The biggest

trick is not wanting anything
too much.

The yard is covered
with townsfolk numbered
like cattle and branded
by fall sun on one side

of their faces. The sky
shines removed and blue
to the heart, true
to its name, like a long-
lost cousin. I could
just cry.

September

The farmers got the call on their CBs and came from all over town, their semis
lined up on the gravel like toys. They blowtorched holes at the bottom of the bin
and used some vacuum thing to suck the grain out faster. Still, it would take a while,
which is why the family sat out in lawn chairs, watching the firemen. Margaret too.
She could not be convinced to wait in the house. Her husband George was somewhere
in the corn, working his way down to the auger when his son-in-law turned it off. He
would be dark, the firemen knew, when they pulled him out, and they tried to stand tight,
shoulder to shoulder, but Margaret, she pushed and broke through like a newborn.

Sand

Today there is snow and no sun.

Years ago, a boy was born across the street, and we took care of him from seven in the mornin until supper, until he was five.

I was eleven and gave him a bottle before walking to school. He fell asleep in my arms while a clown on tv gave prizes to children who could toss ping pong balls into buckets. Some children could do it, some couldn't, and this was all the clown would ever know.

Soon after he left us, he got sick, and by this I mean he would be far away when right in front of you. He couldn't get his colors and could get lost in his sentences. The ball would drop at his feet.

Now he has a device implanted just under the skin of his chest, like a hockey puck or can of chew. He's eighteen.

Today the wind is cold. Coming back from the post office, I find him with his hood up and in his winter boots, sitting in a lawn chair at the intersection of two sidewalks. We talk, and he looks through his lashes. Across the street, men work large machinery, preparing a foundation for the new high school. As I said, there was no sun, and this was right. There was the endless grinding of motors and a great metal claw of rough, difficult movements trying to spread the sand, something a hand might have easily done.

The Solace Is Not the Lullaby But That
Anything Can Be a Lullaby

When the German shopkeeper died, they said, *Go back*
to what you know. So there was math. There was standing
at the stove stirring soup until my father came home.
There were bruised train cars and an untruth,
day and night, shadowing the town's streets.
When authorities found it curled asleep
outside his house, their questions
fell into the dark grass. There was a beating
of silence then, until it was a new quiet
they had to pick up and carry away.

Ice Boat Notes

The seasons are always beating us
to the best ideas. This one's spectrum
siphons to bare, to a naked release
of birds. I know. I followed them
like clues, all the way to where the ground
gets shy, dipping down to little creeks, and a huge gray
tank was already there, rusting in the forest like a submarine.

River

The river is a river again,
its grayish shelves saving
a green stain deep inside.

One large piece of ice the size
of a baby blanket spins,
caught. You can bet
it will break. Or watch it
all day, softening.

Every river gives up
something, even if it's shells
for a small brick factory
making buttons on its bank.

The river is a river again, so try. Trying
is sometimes rewarded. Guess when
the ice will crack. Guess the weight
of this wheel. Guess how many
steps it would take holding one arm
of a dead branch.

The year's first rain will be taken
like collection, confession,
the river spilling over
what it cannot take.

The river is a river again, and all
it ever was is there still: the local
genius's latest scam, the bones of carp
and bluegill, the secrets behind that
woman's skull, busted.

IV

The Heart Is One

The fenceline and I are sharing discoveries.
My latest: if you push something
off a ledge, it falls.
The fenceline is going to be
blown away. It was pretty quiet the day
I stood showing it my large, sad muscles.

Bachelor

On the gravel road north of the house,
I run between fields, out away from town.
Sometimes I hit Rottlers' woods, and risk my way
across a rotting streambed bridge, to eventually
lose juncos darting ahead. Usually I keep running.
Bouillons' black dog leaves their lawn
to pace me in the ditch, though he only goes
so far. I'm alone when I hit Larry Heeren's place,
his tidy farmyard, a single room lit. I wonder if
he's reading. His cows never look up as I pass,
sun burning the horizon, some of that heat trapped
in his front windows.

Homage

Sometimes there is only light, and now it's like a broom of thought
pushing up into an attic for the secret and abandoned, what is yet
more light, warm and achy with September.

Thousands of miles away, where I was a girl, this same light fell
on the sweaty heads of boys trotting up from the practice field,
their cleats the sharp ticking of a warm-bodied engine still working
toward the sweet bruise of night, when they'd leave a dark field
darker, their knuckles cold and busted open, ready to jewel in any light.

We

I understand it now. Sometime after midnight
we snuck from the house, waded
through pasture like a search party, nine of us
under the moon and flowing
in one general direction of creek.

In small enough towns, without even gathering,
girls tend to move like this. We swore
we surrounded something—
held it—a trunk the arms
could reach around.

1979

Plucked from oak bark,
this ring of fur.

This metal twists on glass
to a halt. But here

is some grass
for you, this fly

a screen stretched pregnant
caught. Enjoy

the already dead
heat of the garage. Oh—

and three small holes. Hope,
I'll see you.

V

Nest

: a yesterday like this, mild

: a warm unknown this north, this late

: a smell like Iowa's autumn days, musky
  dying smell of sweet, rich dust

: the urge behind my picking up old washers,
  rusted bolts, and metals' other faded colors in feathers

: a place I didn't even know existed
  until this summer, this grove a chapel of light then, green

: a sense I am somewhere behind me, measuring the grass

: the work of a bird, unaware, it seems

: of the river, the opposite bank

: where something has scared the leaves—
  they're up and away—

: the tree above me still with its seeds,
  its branches dragging the water

Guadalquivir

One river black and oily,
one night to come to the soft door
of you at my mouth and open it.

The years have continued
to drop, like a steady rain,
their tiny stones.

They tower like slim books
stacked in the grass, and over the fence
a weedy lot, a makeshift stage,
a young magician in her cape.

One day, a dark river of vein
will rise through the burn, but now
her hand lies deep in the hat,
wrapped dove-white.

Nest (II)

She's hauled before going

what's the size of a cauldron

and heavy as a body

into the pines,

a quiet mass

of wire, leaves, nearly five

pounds of seed, and down

from one pillow.

Love Affair That Is the Walk Home

Out into the cold, slushy streets, these streets
where a dark lake never leaves the air,
where children are going to bed, their lights
turned out before they can say, *Wait—*
I've forgotten something about you—I'm forgetting
even as you close the door—

tonight I take roads where deer watch you,
and where you watch, breath held
by a house that's all windows, a mother
carrying an infant through lit rooms,
until a door opens and closes and they disappear,
until the deer runs and its young hesitate
then imitate her fleeing.

November Elegy

Who were they, those women

watching the sky

lose heat, while I

with the dark

played, fell to the yard

again and again, the cold then

merely a smell on me.

VI

Storm of the Century

It seems it may be over,
but I found a new way
to the hospital, all while
the day blew around, big
flakes looking gray
against a sky hung
dirty white. A girl
was walking the most
beautiful dog. I heard myself
tell her. The universe
opens up and I do not
fail when it snows. I also found
a shed. It was perfect, its blue
doors dying and so dark I could stand
and see snow coming down,
a movie. Something else beautiful:
I remembered, the town I'm from,
people there went about their day
and work as if they thought
no one was watching.

The Steps in the Snow Lead Around
and Around a Place Called Want

At night the horses rush the fence as sound.
Then as everything else.
I try to sleep beneath the owl now.
My thoughts fly ahead,
swooping back to me
out of breath.
We have seen every edge, they say,
and you were right.

Pony

The day my mother was bowled over by the neighbor's black and white miniature
staked in the field was a day of clarity and a tidy loop like that of an owl,
or an ice rink, or hair being braided.

I found her in a quiet violet-gray at one end of the couch. No light was on her.

The years I spent in the mountains left me unable to recover her face. A sliver
I could grasp at a time, phases of it like a moon's, but never the thing whole.

There is something we take from the violet hour because we need it.
And everything we take resembles what we took before.

I thought it was her father's death that held her those hours normally kept
for us, our supper, our pain. She said she'd tried to hug its neck, to bury
her face in the mane.

The Rain Falls Far

That Easter we painted porcelain rabbits and chicks. We were too young to know what chicks couldn't be, and our mother never said different. She let us paint them blue. She let us slide around on the red linoleum and eat chocolate chip cookie cereal. When you take your family and live in someone else's basement, you take yourself to a new level. Your children playing on a fake black leather couch seem to fall against it like snow. They look to you like snow falling in the house, and it's true—you create a new season, the pool table kept like a corpse, rooms closet-cold. Your youngest two at night sneak up the stairs to find the sculpture sometimes lit: a young boy and girl strolling beneath an umbrella. Your children share the top stair, which is soil-level and also their sky.

Brother

This was long after the sun, and time
a band that played as a great swath of light that ran
ringing the horizon and drew us to it.

We were a different kind of fool then, trimmed
stiff by patterns like stars we might forget
except they held the night and sidewalks through it. And you

with your frog heart beating. This was before I saw boats
as cradles, or bad, before any man
had said they were a graveyard. Now I see us

just before we started to change our course, simple crafts
our ships, our sails
such blankets hung from our arms.

They're Saying Now That Feathers Are Mostly Light,
That Wings Are Mostly Not There

But sometimes it's warm enough for the neighbor
to stand in the field

and brush out her horse's tail. She knows the sun
slips through it.

The horse is two-toned, losing a winter coat, the day
like a world

slipping through its own hands. Dusk will lead them
out to a road

that leads out of town, and she'll teach it how to walk this way,
through shadow.

Vespers

Tonight my neighbor's burning
a fire next to his trailer.

I catch glimpses of his red cap
through the smoke.

The people I've watched die
said, finally, *You smell good*

or *Your hands are cold* or *You've left me*
more confused than ever.

Outside the yard goes black.
My neighbor's wife goes to him

by flashlight, and he bends
to greet the dogs.

Requiem

Across the street, two boys begin to bury
a girl in leaves. Kneeling at her side
they show her how to cover her face—*don't
forget to breathe,* I imagine they tell her,
when what they really should say is, *Try
to remember the smell of sun through it all. It's
a rare courtship.* I watch her help,
gathering the leaves to her like love,
hiding herself. No matter how many, it's
the same heavy. One leaf will find its way
beneath her shirt, another will tickle her lip.
What she'll hear is almost like breathing,
and it must be the leaves. Sounds beyond love,
sounds beyond love . . . Remember, I would tell her,
there are such things.

Shell Rock Song

It's less important why
and more important where
we leave some things.

I should have learned
this by now, grown
in a small river town,

collecting, as a girl,
colored stones from clear,
shallow depths. Before

home, they'd have dried
themselves dull. They left
my pockets wet.

Today at the river
only the geese were there,
held in glare of winter sun.

Again I tried to take
the shape of solitude
at the side of a river.

Again I stood motionless,
yet they were more still.
I stayed, adoring them,

over an hour in the cold,
waiting, I think,
for them to love me.

Then I walked home.

Acknowledgments

The author gratefully acknowledges the publications where these poems originally appeared:

Alaska Quarterly Review "From" and "Vespers"

Beloit Poetry Journal "Lake Saganaga" and "Pony"

Big Muddy: A Journal of the Mississippi River Valley "Shell Rock Song" (as "To a Fisherman, After Years")

Black Warrior Review "The Steps in the Snow Lead Around and Around a Place Called Want"

The Chattahoochee Review "Homage"

The Cincinnati Review "The Rain Falls Far"

Copper Nickel "Storm of the Century"

Crazyhorse "Brother"

Cream City Review "Fall"

The Georgia Review "They're Saying Now That Feathers Are Mostly Light, That Wings Are Mostly Not There"

The Gettysburg Review "Mars"

Granta (granta.com) "Requiem"

Green Mountains Review "The Horses Are Fighting"

The Iowa Review "Edge of the World," "Some Roads in Iowa," and "Some Roads in Iowa (II)" (as part of "Some Roads in Iowa")

New Letters "Chances of Finding a Heart at an Auction," "Of Unsent Letters, One," and "We" (as "Sara Litterer's Birthday")

Ninth Letter "Sand"

Ploughshares "On Death"

Prairie Schooner "This Field Wasn't Always a Field"

Quarterly West "Ice Boat Notes" and "The Solace Is Not the Lullaby But That Anything Can Be a Lullaby"

The Southern Review "Bachelor," "Grip," "The Heart Is One," "Nest (II)," "November Elegy," "Relume," and "River"
String Poet (stringpoet.com) "Nest" and "Without"
Subtropics "Guadalquivir" and "Love Affair That Is the Walk Home"
32 Poems "Kansas" and "September"
ZYZZYVA "Small Town"